The Roots of True Faith

D1289141

The Roots of True Faith

William Guthrie

An abridged version, re-written for today's readers, of the
classic 'The Christian's Great Interest' by William Guthrie
(1620-1665). The full version is published by the
'Banner of Truth Trust'.

Prepared by Roger Devenish

Root: ...the essential substance and nature of something; the
basis of something...
The Concise Oxford Dictionary, 1990 reprint.

© GRACE PUBLICATIONS TRUST
175 Tower Bridge Road
London SE1 2AH
England
e-mail: AGBCSE@AOL.com

First published 1992
2nd Impression 1998

ISBN 0 946462 28 3

Distributed by:
EVANGELICAL PRESS
Grange Close
Faverdale North
Darlington DL3 OPH
England

Printed in Great Britain by
Creative Print and Design (Wales), Ebbw Vale

Cover design: L.L. Evans

'The author I take to have been one of the greatest divines that ever wrote; it always goes with me. I have written several folios, but there is more divinity in it than in them all.'

John Owen, 1616-1683

'... I still think it the best composition I ever read relating to a subject in which we are all deeply interested, and about which it is my earnest prayer that we may all be found on the right side of the question.'

Thomas Chalmers, 1780-1847.

To The Reader*

Most people, in these days, make it very clear by their behaviour that they have no wish to choose Christ and the everlasting blessings that are in him. In this little book I have tried to show you what is the Christian's great interest; think about it seriously!

You may be surprised to see anything from my pen; indeed, I surprise myself by writing! But I have had to do it, for some rough notes of a few sermons of mine have been published, which were poorly edited and put together in a confusing way. That has made me attempt this work.

I have purposely written simply, and briefly, for I know that the persons for whom I write have not much money to buy books, nor much time to read them.

You may find things here to be critical of. I have no wish to offend anyone. I only hope to write what will be helpful to you, and what will perhaps prompt others more able than I, to write in greater detail.

Your servant in the work of the Gospel,

William Guthrie, 1658.

----

*Guthrie's original has been re-written for today's readers.

Contents

Part One —
Who is a Christian?

1.
Being sure about our salvation

What makes someone a Christian? Perhaps you have asked that question. You may even have asked it about yourself. 'Am I a Christian? Can I be sure that Jesus Christ has saved me from sin? Do I really love God?'

We can easily think we know the answers to these questions, yet we need to be cautious. Jesus Christ himself warns us that we can be mistaken. Think of what he said, as we read it in Matthew chapter 7 verses 22 and 23. There Jesus says that many people will tell him they prophesied in his name, or cast out demons, or did many wonders. Nevertheless, Jesus will tell them, 'I never knew you.'

It follows that we need to be sure that Jesus has accepted us. We need to know whether we are Christian believers. In this book I want to help you do that.

Let me make the point first of all, that we *can* know for certain that Jesus Christ has saved us from sin, and made us his people. It is easier to be sure of this than some people think. For one thing, God tells us in the Bible that we can find out whether we belong to Jesus Christ. 'Examine yourselves to see if you are in the faith,' God says to us (2 Corinthians 13:5). Then the apostle Paul tells us he is sure that nothing can separate him from the love of God (Romans 8:38-39). So we *can* know for sure that God loves us. David, in the old Testament, was certain of this, too. See what he says, in Psalm 27 verse 1, 'The Lord is my light and my salvation. Whom shall I fear?'

If you are not sure whether God is your saviour, think of it like this. All who receive Jesus Christ are called the children of God; 'to those who received him he gave power to become children of God' (John 1:12). Have you received Christ in the way the Bible speaks of receiving him? Do you believe that Christ died in place of sinners, himself bearing God's anger against their sin, instead of them? Do you know that you are a sinner? Have you turned away from all sin? Have you turned to Jesus Christ as your King to rule over you, as your Priest to pray for you, and as your Prophet to teach you? Are you resting and relying on Jesus Christ alone to bring you to God? Do you want to thank him and please him with all your heart and all your being? Well – what more can be meant by receiving Christ? If you have received Christ like that, the Bible assures you that you belong to God — you are one of his children.

I want to say how important it is to know that God has saved us. Our very life depends upon it. Yet Jesus warns us that the gate which leads to life is small and the way is narrow, and there are only a few that find it (Matthew 7:14). So it's important to be sure we *are* on that way to life.

If we want to be sure, we must let the Bible teach us. The Bible is the rule which must guide us. If the Bible makes it clear that you belong to God — then accept it gladly. On the other hand, if the Bible shows you clearly that you are not a true Christian — do not try to hide from the truth. There is no other guide to the truth than the Bible, as the holy Spirit helps us to understand it.

In conclusion, we know if we are Christian believers. We can be sure that we belong to God. And it is most important that we know whether or not we are saved by Jesus Christ.

How is it, then, that so many people are uncertain about these things? Perhaps you yourself are not really sure. 'Am I a Christian?' you may perhaps often ask. 'I think perhaps I am, but I'm not certain.' Well, many people are unsure like that. Why? Let me suggest a few reasons.

First, people do not know about God and his ways of doing things. They do not realise that God did not have to send Jesus Christ into the world. There was nothing about us that made him do it. God did it because he loved us, not because we deserved it. ' God so loved the world, that he gave his one and only Son' (John 3:16). There was no reason for God to love us. In fact, one of the first things a real Christian learns is that there is nothing good in him at all. Sin affects everything about him. That's why the real Christian makes so much of Jesus Christ. He is the only one who is good. He is the only one who can do us good. He alone can forgive our sin and bring us to know God. So the true Christian lives now to please the Lord Jesus, and to become like him in character. This is God's way of doing things. If we do not know about this way, we can never be certain whether we are Christians. The Christian's hope is all in God. God alone can save sinners.

However, some people are unsure whether they are Christians because they do not know that God deals with people in different ways. They forget that people come to Christ by different means, and at different speeds. Zacchaeus came to Jesus Christ at once when Jesus called him (you can read about that at the start of Luke 19). Paul had to wait for three days (as we find in Acts 9). One person's experience of coming to faith in Jesus differs from another's. There is no one pattern which, in itself, makes you a Christian.

In the same way, no two Christians are equally holy. Some live very good lives. Others make sad mistakes and at times do what is wrong. Some enjoy God's blessing and seem to be friends of God in a special way. Others enjoy far less of this nearness to God. Even so, all are true believers.

Secondly, we can be unsure about whether we are Christians because we are not honest with God. If we are holding on to some sin, though we know it is wrong, and if we are not asking God's forgiveness and his help to fight against evil, then no wonder we are unsure whether we belong to God. If we are refusing to do what God says is right, we will be confused about whether we love God.

Thirdly, if we don't really *want* to know whether we are real Christians, it is not surprising that we are confused about it all. We need to make some effort to see if we are born again. 'Examine yourselves to see if you are in the faith: test yourselves', said Paul (2 Corinthians 13:5). We must work hard at this, says Peter (2 Peter 1:10) 'be eager to make sure of these things,' he says. If we spend all our time on our own interests, and are not even trying to settle this important question, no wonder we are still confused.

Fourthly, some people look for the wrong signs of being a Christian. Then because they cannot see these signs in themselves, they wonder whether they belong to God. For instance, some people think that real Christians can never sin. And then, because they themselves sin, they think they cannot be Christians. Yet the Bible shows that Christians sin from time to time. The apostle Paul describes his life as a struggle with sin (Romans 7:14-25). In the same way, others think that true Christians always receive direct answers to their prayers. But this is not a sign of a true believer. See what the Psalmist says in Psalm 13:1: 'How long will you forget me, O Lord? For ever? How long will you hide your face from me?' Still others expect a special sense of the holy Spirit, telling them they belong to God, as Romans chapter 8 verse 16 describes: 'The Spirit himself witnesses with our spirit that we are the children of God'. But they forget that believing in Jesus Christ comes first, and only then does the holy Spirit assure us we belong to God; 'having believed, you were sealed with the holy Spirit' (Ephesians 1:13). If we look for such signs of being a Christian, which are not really signs at all, we are going to be confused about whether we belong to God.

I hope you can see by now that it is important for us to know whether we are right with God, and that we can be sure about this. I hope you can see, too, why people are confused about being a Christian. They forget that salvation is God's gift, and not something they deserve. They forget that God deals with people in a great many ways: quickly with some, more slowly with others. They forget that true Christians differ in holiness; they look for signs of being a Christian which are not true of all Christian people.

May I mention some other mistakes people make about being a Christian?

Firstly, a person can belong to God, yet not know it. The apostle John said; 'I have written these things to you who believe, so that you may know that you have eternal life' (1 John 5:13). This suggests that there were people who did not know that they had God's life in them.

Secondly, not everyone is equally certain about belonging to Christ. One person may only feel able to say, 'Lord, I do believe: help my unbelief' (Mark 9:24). Paul, however, could say, 'Nothing can separate us from the love of God' (Romans 8:38-39). In the same way, the confidence of Christians can change: it does not always remain at the same strength.

Thirdly, true Christians cannot always answer all the arguments against their faith, yet all Christians will always know they believe Christ; 'I know whom I have believed' (2 Timothy 1:12).

There is also a false confidence in Christ. Parables like that of the wise and foolish virgins, at the start of Matthew chapter 25, teach us that many can appear to be true Christians, but have no real, personal faith in Jesus Christ.

I hope you can see that we need to be sure we are genuine Christians — and that we *can* be sure of that.

2.
Ways in which people are drawn to Christ

In this chapter I want to talk about the different ways in which people are called to faith in Jesus Christ. People are not all drawn to Jesus in the same way. We need to remember this. We must not expect that our experience of coming to Christ will be just the same as someone else's.

Some people, for instance, are called by God very early in their lives. Timothy seems to have been such a person. We find (2 Timothy 3:15) that from his childhood Timothy had known the Scriptures. John the Baptist was filled with the holy Spirit from his birth (Luke 1:15). God called Timothy and John the Baptist to be his people, very early in their lives. And so it may be with some people now. There are people whom God saves in their childhood, God keeps them from many sins, and Christianity seems almost natural to them. They do not have to be made to pray, or listen to Christian teaching, or do God's will. They already love these things and are interested in them. People who come to Christ in early years may not know exactly when they became believers, but they know when God speaks to them in some special way, and they know when God calls them to greater obedience to him. Such people can be sure that God has called them to believe in him from their youth.

Other people come to faith in Christ very suddenly and quickly. They find that God loves them and is calling them to himself. This happened to Zacchaeus. Christ simply called him, and immediately he left everything else to follow him (Luke 19). Notice, though, that Zacchaeus already wanted to see Christ — he was even ready to look ridiculous, climbing a tree to see Jesus. And remember, too, that Jesus spoke to his heart; what Jesus said took hold of Zacchaeus so deeply that he was glad to trust in the Saviour. Also, Zacchaeus was changed by coming to Jesus: once he had been greedy, but now he cared about the poor and the people he had cheated. Zacchaeus knew he had done wrong. All these things were signs that Jesus had saved him, even though he came to Christ very silently.

Zacchaeus shows us that people are not always concerned about their sin, or about God's holiness or God's commandments, before they come to Christ. Some people are concerned about these things. They spend a long time discovering how guilty they are in God's sight, before ever they are converted, but it does not *have* to be like this in every case, as Zacchaeus shows us.

Others come to Christ when they are near to death. The thief on the cross, of whom we read in Luke chapter 23 verses 40 to 43, was like this. Although he came to Christ as he was dying, he came truly. There is no doubt that God saved him. This thief was different from the other: he told him that Jesus had done nothing wrong. He knew that he was being punished justly, and he knew that Jesus was not guilty. He realised that Jesus was a king, even though he was hanging on a cross. He believed in a place of glory after death, and was more interested in that than in this present life. He trusted himself to Christ's mercy, and knew that if only Jesus remembered him, it would be all he needed. All these things show us that the thief who turned to Christ at the time of his death, now truly belonged to God.

So the thief shows us that some people come to Christ at the very point of death. Such people, though, are few. We need to listen to God's call to repent now, while we are healthy, and not delay.

Some people, then, are called to God almost from birth. Others come to Christ suddenly, drawn by the love of the Lord Jesus. A few come to him as death approaches. But usually people are prepared for Christ by realising they are sinners, by being troubled in their consciences, and by seeing that they are completely helpless and under God's judgement.

Even in cases like this, there are differences in the speed at which God works. Some become aware that they are sinners very suddenly, like the Apostle Paul or the jailer at Philippi. They realise they cannot do anything to save themselves — like the jailer (Acts 16:30); 'What must I do to be saved?' They are ready for God's salvation on God's terms and in God's way. And they show a change in their lives by joining with other Christians, just as Paul did after his conversion. This is what happens when people suddenly realise that they are sinners.

But sometimes these things happen over a long period of time, so slowly that they are hardly noticed. Gradually God shows people that they are sinners. Some part of the Bible, some preaching, some thought arising in their minds, makes them see that they are guilty before God. Slowly they realise that they are guilty not just of some sins, but of many. Then they understand that they are full of sin. So the holy Spirit comes and convinces them of sin (John 16:8).

Then God shows such people that appearing to be religious is not enough. We cannot pretend we have faith in Christ, when we have not really believed in him. The Spirit convinces such people of sin because they have not believed on the Son of God (John 16:9).

Thus people are brought to care about their salvation. The question on their minds is, 'What must I do to be saved?' 'What shall it profit a man, to gain the whole world and lose his own soul?' (Matthew 16:26) they ask. Some people even become so concerned about their sin that they are afraid to die, or fear that they have sinned against the holy Spirit.

At this point, God quietly puts thoughts of mercy into the minds of such people. They see that God has been merciful to great sinners, and that God receives all who submit to Jesus Christ, whatever they may have been in the past.

This knowledge that God saves sinners makes people more eager to seek salvation. Sometimes they even think that they can do enough to earn their salvation, but God shows them that no-one can serve the Lord like that, 'for he is a holy God and a jealous God' (Joshua 24:19). God makes them more aware than ever of their sinfulness — and how sin affects even the very best they can do.

Often, at this point, people want to be alone and think. They think how foolish it is to fight against God; how often they might have turned to God; how happy Christians are in being at peace with God, and how patient and merciful God has been to them.

In this way they make up their minds to pray to God for mercy, and as they pray now they really mean it when they call themselves sinners. They want answers to their prayers, and seem to be listening for them. They are eagerly seeking now for God to have mercy on them and assure them that he is their saviour. They are prepared for true faith in the Lord Jesus.

Now I am not saying that all these things happen to every person who comes to faith in Christ over a period of time. But where things such as these happen, it is usual to find people being saved by God's grace.

Of course people can be troubled by sin without any good coming of it, but usually there are differences between this and the true work of God. When God works, concern about one sin leads to concern about another — and then to concern about all kinds of sin. When God is at work, people come to see that they are sinners and that they are specially guilty in his sight. Those who are just troubled about some specially noticeable sins, never come to see themselves like this. Indeed, they usually think that in many ways they are better than others, and certainly do not think that sin is like a disease inside them. They will even forget about the few sins that trouble them, when something more interesting gains their attention! Where God is at work in people's lives, however, they have no peace till they find his mercy.

Perhaps, as you have seen so far, you have thought that you are not deeply enough troubled by your sins. You may be asking, 'Have I had a thorough enough sight of my sin and need? Am I ready to believe in the Lord Jesus?'

Let me simply ask you four questions. Firstly, do you know that you can never save yourself from sin? Do you know that you *must* have Jesus Christ to save you, and that he came 'to seek and to save what was lost' (Luke 19:10)?

Secondly, do you know that you need the Lord Jesus Christ, and *only* Jesus Christ, to save you and bring you to God? Do you value the Lord Jesus above all else?

Thirdly, do you want to leave all sin behind, to turn away from it, to hate it, and to fight against it? 'Come out from among then and be separate, says the Lord. Do not touch what is unclean, and I will receive you' (2 Corinthians 6:17).

Fourthly, do you want to do *all* that God says to you, thankfully and obediently?

If God has brought you to know that you have no spiritual goodness; if Jesus Christ is all that you need; if God has taught you to turn from all sin; and if God has led you to want to do his will — then you are truly seeking God and his salvation!

3.
Evidence that a person is a Christian

Are you a Christian? That's the question I'm asking you to think about in this book. I want you to ask yourself how you can be sure that Jesus Christ is your saviour, and that God's mercy has come to you. In earlier chapters I've said that we *can* know these things — and we've looked at the different ways in which God works to bring people to himself.

Now I want to describe some even clearer signs that show if a person is a Christian believer. Faith is one such sign, for faith is necessary if we are to be saved from sin. As Paul and Silas told the jailer at Philippi, '*Believe on* the Lord Jesus Christ, and you will be saved' (Acts chapter 16:31).

Yet people sometimes think that faith is a mysterious thing — so strange and mysterious that they can never reach it. To such people I would say: faith is not so difficult as many think it is. Yes — faith is God's gift, and we cannot produce it. But, 'If you confess with your mouth that Jesus is Lord, and believe in your heart that God raised him from the dead, you will be saved' (Romans 10:9). Read the whole passage in Romans chapter 10, verses 5 to 13, and you will see that Paul is saying that faith is not a difficult thing. Faith is really a matter of the will and the heart. It means being drawn to Jesus Christ, resting and relying upon him, leaning on him and finding our treasure in him. Faith is a matter of wanting Jesus Christ, and looking to him for salvation from sin. It means receiving Jesus Christ in this way. John tells us, 'To all who received him, to those who believed on his name, he gave the right to become children of God' (John 1:12). Faith means coming to Christ with a longing for him. 'All that the Father gives me will come to me,' said Jesus (John 6:37) 'and the one who comes to me I will never turn away.' Faith means looking to Christ and wanting his salvation, 'Turn to me and be saved, all you ends of the earth' (Isaiah 45:22).

So faith, as I am speaking of it now, is not difficult. Faith does not mean understanding difficult things about God. Faith does not, first of all, mean believing that God has chosen *me*, or that God loves *me*, or that Christ died for *me*. Such things are truly difficult. But the faith which brings us into God's blessing is none of these things. The faith which brings us into salvation is a matter of wanting Christ, being drawn to Christ, leaning upon him and trusting him.

Even so, for some people, such saving faith is too much to claim. They tell us it is being too confident if people say they are drawn to Jesus Christ. Yet, if we are to be saved at all, we must have this faith which comes to Jesus Christ and will not let him go. Without this trusting faith, nothing else will do. Unless we believe, we are still condemned by God. 'He who does not believe is condemned already because he has not believed in the name of the one and only Son of God' (John 3:18). So saving faith is not too much to claim. If we cannot claim it, we have no hope at all.

Nevertheless, people still say that we cannot be sure we have faith. John, however, tells us in his first letter that the person who believes has a witness in himself (1 John 5:10). In other words, we *can* know that we are trusting in Christ. How can we know this? Well, in the last chapter I explained that we will often find that God has prepared us for faith. We become convinced that we are lost. We see that we cannot save ourselves from sin. We realise that Christ alone is able to save us completely. We know that this is the one thing that can do us good. Preparation like this often comes before true faith.

And other things come with this true faith. If we are trusting in Christ, we will want him to rule our lives; we will learn from his teaching; we will want to give ourselves to him whole-heartedly. All these things come along with true faith, and others besides, But, though all these things are evidence to us, I must still say that we can normally know in ourselves, by the ordinary help of the Holy Spirit, whether we have faith in the Lord Jesus Christ.

Perhaps it will help you if I say a little more about what this faith is like. It is described in the Bible in various ways — because faith is experienced in different ways by different people. Sometimes faith is described as wanting to be united to God and at peace with God. Isaiah calls this 'looking to God': 'Look unto me and be saved, all you ends of the earth' (Isaiah 45:22). *Looking* may seem a very weak act of faith, for we may look at what we dare not approach, or dare not touch; we may look at someone to whom we dare not speak. Yet God has promised that those who look to him in faith will be saved from sin. This shows itself simply as looking to God, as wanting to be at one with God. This is the faith the Bible talks about when it speaks of 'willing': 'Whoever will (whoever wishes) let him take the water of life freely' (Revelation 22:17). This faith that looks to God is also described as 'hungering and thirsting after righteousness' (Matthew 5:6).

Sometimes faith is described as 'leaning on the Lord', or 'resting' on Jesus Christ. It is spoken of as trusting God. Isaiah tells us that God will keep in perfect peace those whose minds are fixed on him, because they trust in him (Isaiah 26:3).

Faith is also described as 'waiting for God'. God has promised, 'They that wait for me shall not be disappointed' (Isaiah 49:23). Indeed, the Bible shows us clearly that Christ can do good to sinners in whatever way they need. Faith draws us to Christ in every way that he is described: when we hear of Christ as the bread of life, faith hungers for him; when we hear

25

of Christ raised from the dead, faith believes that God has raised him. Faith believes on the name of Jesus, in all the different ways that Jesus is described.

Let me repeat, though, that not everybody experiences faith in the same way or to the same extent. In the New Testament Jesus spoke of certain people as having great faith. One case in point is the centurion (Matthew 8:10). From such sayings of Jesus we can see that while others had true faith, not all had great faith. So do not think that faith has to show itself in all the ways I've described, in order to be real faith.

Remember, too, that faith varies in its strength, even in the same person. Sometimes a person's faith is strong and can be easily seen; then it becomes weak, and unbelief grows stronger.

Faith, then, shows itself in various ways; but what is at the heart of true faith is this: to be pleased and satisfied with God's plan of salvation through Jesus Christ. When anyone is thankful for Christ's death in place of sinners, (which means that God can, in justice, forgive sinners) then that person *has* the faith that saves sinners. Saving faith means giving up all thought of ever working to earn God's favour, and resting instead on what Christ has done to bear the penalty due to sin. This faith is in everyone who has been born again — in every true Christian — even though that faith may not show itself in all the ways I've spoken about.

So the question we need to ask ourselves is simply this: Am I satisfied with the Lord Jesus Christ? Is he the one that I value more than anything else? Is he precious to me, because he is the only way to God? Being satisfied with Jesus Christ as our sin-bearer and our only saviour, *is* true faith. For this is believing with the heart. It is being satisfied with God's way of saving sinners through Christ; it is agreeing to God's way of salvation, and receiving it gladly, through Jesus Christ. And let me repeat, we can know if we have faith like this. For we can have no doubt about it if we are resting entirely on Jesus Christ to bring us to God, and if we value Jesus Christ above everyone and everything else. He who believes like this shall not perish, 'but have everlasting life' (John 3:16).

But is it possible to have a false faith which is like true faith — so much like it that we cannot tell the difference? After all, many people admire Jesus today, just as many believed in him when they saw the miracles he did. How can we tell this false, imitation faith, from genuine, true faith?

Firstly, false faith never quite gives up the idea that we can at least help a little in our salvation from sin. False faith makes people ask, like the man in Luke 10:25, 'What must I do to inherit eternal life?' False faith also wants to hold on to other things than Christ alone. So false faith never completely trusts in Christ, and only Christ.

Secondly, people with false faith do not want Christ to rule over them, or to make peace between them and God *at all times,* or to teach and guide them. False faith does not really receive Christ as king and priest and prophet.

Thirdly, false faith is not ready to follow Christ through hardship or loss or suffering. Real faith wants Christ alone, *whatever the cost.*

In the chapters that follow I shall explain other differences between false and true faith. For example, only true faith has the effect of purifying the *inner* life of a person (Acts 15:9). And wherever there is true faith there will always be all the other spiritual virtues as well (Galatians 5:22-23).

4.
More evidence that a person is a Christian

How we can know if someone is a Christian is the question I'm asking you to think about in this book. We *can* know if we belong to God: there are signs which show whether we are born again. One of these signs is faith, which means wanting Jesus Christ and valuing him above everything else, as our Saviour, our King and our Teacher.

Now I want to write about another sign that someone is a Christian. True Christians are *new people*. They have been made new. 'If anyone is in Christ, he is a new creation,' (2 Corinthians 5:17). And in Colossians 3;10 a Christian is described as a 'new person'. In every Christian there is a new kind of life, which wants to be more and more godly. The Christian is a new person who wants to grow in godliness, and to be more like God in character. This is a very clear sign of Christian life.

We can see clearly if someone has this new life from God because it affects every part of that person. When a person is truly a Christian his understanding is affected. A Christian has a new way of thinking. He does not simply think about Christian teachings: he trusts them, relies on them and knows that his life depends on their truth. A Christian does not think of Christian teachings as things to be discussed or argued about — he knows that Christian teaching is sure and certain, something to live for and to die for.

The way a believer understands life is new, too, because he

now sees signs of God's work all around him in the world. The Christian sees God at work in the ordinary affairs of life, holding back evil and working for good. He sees God's work in the creation around him — in the sky and on the earth. The Christian is also sensitive to the work of God in other people's lives and in his own life as well.

Furthermore, in addition to the mind, the desires of the Christian are made new. The driving force of his life changes. Unbelievers have 'hearts of stone' — they do not care about God — their hearts are hard towards God. But when God converts a person, that person is given a new set of attitudes – he or she is driven along by new desires and intentions. The Christian now wants to please God, and to keep his laws. The Christian wants to care for other Christians, and to do good to them. The Christian's heart is stirred up against sin, and against everything God says is wrong. This new driving force in the Christian's life, takes pleasure in God himself, in God's law and in God's people. This is how Ezekiel describes this new heart, 'I will give you a new heart and put a new spirit in you. I will take the stony heart from you and I will give you a heart of flesh. And I will put my Spirit in you and lead you to follow my commandments, and you will keep my laws and do them,' (Ezekiel 36:26,27).

Do you have a heart for God, for his people and for his commandments? This is a part of being a new kind of person — and that is part of being a Christian. Indeed, this change even affects our bodies, for we once used our tongues, our eyes, our ears, our hands and our feet for sinful purposes, but now we want to do what is good and pleasing to God, with our bodies.

This change, this renewing, which is part of being a Christian, affects *every part* of the believer's life to some extent at least. When we are united to Jesus Christ, 'all things become new' (2 Corinthians 5:17).

Our interests change for the better. Once we were interested in whatever was to our own advantage. We wanted to do well for ourselves, and were ready to get everything we wanted, but now our interests have changed: we want to please the Lord Jesus Christ, and to see his kingdom prosper. We want to do well for him.

Our worship also becomes new. Before, if we worshipped God, it was out of habit, or duty. Perhaps we had been brought up to worship God, but our hearts were never in it. Our worship meant nothing to us personally, but now, if God has saved us, this has changed, too. Our worship is helped by the holy Spirit. We worship in Spirit and in truth, as Jesus himself described it (John 4:23). Though we often fail to worship God as we would like, there is something sincere and genuine in our worship which was not there before.

The way we do our work and think about our duties is renewed. We now want to be, as Romans chapter 12 verse 11 says, 'Not lazy in business, but eager in spirit, serving the Lord.' We want to do everything in our work and in our daily tasks in order to please God and to bring him praise. And at work, too, whenever we can, we want to remember that God is with us, and to speak to him in prayer.

Our relationships with other people are renewed. We want to be better husbands, fathers, brothers, mothers, sisters and neighbours.

In addition, our use of the blessings of this life is changed for the better. If we are blessed with food, drink, sleep, recreation or clothes, then we want to use these things to please God. We do not want these blessings to take up all our time and attention. We do not want our food, or our drink or our clothes to become all-important. We want to be self-controlled in the way we use these blessings.

So when we are Christians, we are different in every way. We could sum it all up by saying that we want to become holy. If we truly want to *please* God, we can be assured that we *belong* to God. For our conscience will tell us that we want to keep God's commandments. And John teaches us that this is a sign that we know God: 'We know that we have come to know him, if we keep his commandments,' (1 John 2:3).

The question which we need to answer, then, is this: Do I keep God's commandments? If I do, this is a sign of God's new life in me. It is a sign that I am born again and have been made a new kind of person. So, do I keep those commands that forbid sin? Do I fight against secret sins, and sins which might be thought unimportant? Do I guard against failing to do what I should do, as well as against doing wrong? (For not doing what is right is as much a sin as doing evil). Do I take care to avoid the sins which I am personally very likely to commit? (For we all have sins which we can easily fall into, because of our nature and our temperament). The true Christian fights hard against all sins, works hard to avoid all evil, and wants to do all possible good. This is the effect of God's new life in the believer. It is a sign that he is a renewed person. The Christian respects all God's commandments, and wants to obey God's will more and more completely. This is the way of holiness — and it shows that we belong to God, and that his new life has been given to us.

Maybe all this talk of holiness seems beyond you. 'It's too hard for ordinary people,' you might think, but remember, God himself has promised to give his people the strength and power to seek for holiness and to be holy. It is God who has said he will take away our stony hearts and give us hearts to reverence him. He has promised to put his law in our hearts and to give us his holy Spirit. God, who gives new life to sinners, also gives them the strength to live a new life, for him.

Remember, too, that not all Christians show this new life to the same extent. In some believers the new life is very plain for all to see. In others, it is there, but not so clearly. As I've said before, no two Christian believers are quite the same: some show very clear signs of new life; others show the new life less plainly.

Even so, we must be clear that all true believers have new life from God, and that this life can be seen. If you doubt this, read Ephesians chapter 4 verses 20 to 24. In verse 20 Paul writes to those who had come to know Christ, i.e. to Christian believers. But how can we see that someone knows Christ? Paul goes on to write about taking off our old, sinful way of life — our old sinful nature, our old habits — in the same way that we take off our clothes. In other words, the new life can be seen when we turn away from sin and evil. Then Paul adds that we are to put on a new nature, which is made to be like God in goodness and holiness. The new life can be seen when Christian people make every effort to be like God in their character — to be just and pure and good. There must be something in every part of the Christian's life which points towards God. We cannot always see this in ourselves — but if we could see how God is changing us we should see that we are not now what we once were. There is a difference in our lives, and there must be a difference, if we are Christians. God's new life in a person shows itself in growth towards holiness.

We must be clear, too, that nobody who has this new life can live comfortably with sin. Once a Christian understands that something is sinful, he will turn from it. There can be no agreement between sin and someone made new by God's grace.

One thing must be kept in mind at this point. As I ask you whether you have the signs of God's new life, please judge yourself by your *normal* state of living. Christians do sometimes fall into sin — and at such times we can wonder if we have any signs of God's new life. Don't think of yourself as you are at such times, but as you are in the ordinary course of your life. In conclusion, as you consider your normal pattern of living, are there the signs of holiness and a changed life? Every true Christian is a changed person.

5.
Differences between true and false faith

So far I've said that it is possible to know if we are believers in the Lord Jesus Christ. Faith in Christ is not something we need be unsure about. A true Christian is a new person: someone who has new life from God. If anyone is changed like that, we can see it. The Christian's new life shows itself. In particular, the Christian sees that Jesus Christ is above everything else: Christ is the most important, the most precious person to the believer. The Christian also wants to please God in every part of life, and to keep God's commandments. Changes like this help us to see whether a person is born again.

'But surely', you may say, 'other people too, can be changed. Many people admire Jesus Christ. Many people want to live in a Christian way. Are you saying that all these people are true Christian believers?'

Well, it's certainly true that people can look like Christians but not have God's new life in them. This is sad but true, and it's what I want to explain in this chapter. I believe that there are differences between true Christians and people who seem to be Christian believers, but are not.

First of all, let me say that these two sorts of people can seem to be very much alike. It is possible to seem to be a Christian, yet not really to be changed and made new. For instance, both true Christians and those who only seem to be Christians can have much knowledge about the faith. As Hebrews chapter 6 verse 4 puts it, 'they have been enlightened.'

You may not be a true Christian, yet you may have great understanding of Christian beliefs. You may even get very excited about Christian teaching. Like the stony ground in Christ's parable, you can receive the word of God with joy (Matthew 13:20). You can change your way of life, avoid sin, and do what is right just like the Pharisee who rightly said, 'God, I thank you I am not like other people' (Luke 18:11). You can approve of Christ's teaching, like those who said of Jesus in John chapter 7 verse 46, 'No-one ever spoke like this man.' You can be like this, yet not be a true Christian.

In the same way, people who are not true Christians can sound very much like believers. They may talk about the gospel, they may admit their sinfulness to others, they may be sorry for their sin, they may learn what God wants them to do, they may join with Christians for a time and work with them, they may give money to God's work. They may do all this, yet not be true Christians.

Also, people who are not really Christians may become painfully aware of their sin. They can be worried about the evil in themselves, just as Judas was when he said, 'I have sinned because I have betrayed innocent blood' (Matthew 27:4). They may be deeply troubled when they hear preaching about God's holiness, and his judgement to come against evil, and the need for self-control and holiness of life. Felix was like this, when Paul preached to him: as Paul reasoned about righteousness, self-control and judgement, Felix was afraid (Acts 24:25). Later, these same people, who are troubled by God's truth, may find some peace and quiet, expecting Christ to save them. And all this may be followed by a good deal of reformation in character and change in ways of life. Indeed, all this concern for sin and change of conduct may seem to be strengthened by some special experiences of God's goodness. Hebrews chapter 6 verses 4 and 5 even shows that such people can find a certain kind of enjoyment in what God says. Yet, despite all this, they may still be far from God, unchanged by God's blessing of new life.

Such people may even have signs which are very much like the holy Spirit's work in true believers. The holy Spirit gives faith, and you can have a sort of faith, yet not be a true believer. Simon Magus 'also believed,' it says, 'and when he was baptized he followed Philip everywhere and was amazed at the signs and miracles that were done' (Acts 8:13). You can also have a sort of repentance, or a sense of wonder and fear before God, yet not be a true believer. I would say that everything the holy Spirit gives to the believer can be imitated by people who are not true believers.

It is even possible, I believe, for people to have experiences very much like those of true Christians, and yet not to be changed by any true work of God in their lives. People can know something of the power of the holy Spirit at work in them and yet not really be changed into God's people. I think this is what the writer of the letter to the Hebrews is talking about when he says that people who have understood something of God's truth, and have tasted the heavenly gift, who have shared in the holy Spirit, who have tasted the goodness of the word of God and powers of the coming age, cannot be brought back to repentance if they fall away, (Hebrews 6:4,5).

So then, if unbelievers can look so much like believers, how can we tell the difference?

One important difference is that the true believer's inner life is changed and made new. This never happens with someone who simply looks like a Christian, but is not. True Christianity begins in our hearts. By that I mean that the real change takes place at the centre of our life. There is a deep change in our thinking, in what we want, and in how we feel. That is what Ezekiel meant when he said that God would give his people a heart of flesh in place of a stony heart (Ezekiel 36:26). He meant that God would change the way they thought and felt, and change their wills to want what God wanted. The true Christian *is* changed like this. In particular, the true Christian knows that Jesus Christ is the only satisfying blessing in all the world, for whom it is worthwhile to leave everything else behind. The real believer knows that 'the kingdom of heaven is like treasure hidden in a field: when man has found it he hides it again and for the sheer joy of it goes and sells all he has, to buy that field'. (Matthew 13:44). If you have been made new by God's grace you will know that a deep change has taken place in you, so that you find in Jesus Christ alone everything that is good and worthwhile.

This leads to the second difference between a true Christian and someone who simply looks like a Christian, but is not. People who are not real Christians may change their way of living and say they are new people, but these changes do not come from a change of heart or from wanting to please God. There is always, instead, some other aim in mind. Perhaps they want to win the praise of other people for their lives. Perhaps they hope to escape God's anger against their sin. They may wish to get themselves out of some trouble, or to be set free from a guilty conscience. Whatever it is, the aim will always be something other than pleasing God. Only the true Christian wants to please God. Only the born again person will 'seek first the kingdom of God and his righteousness' (Matthew 6:33). The one thing that is needed for a true Christian life is having Christ as our friend and our companion. But this is the one thing which those who are not true believers never really want to have.

I said a little while ago that people who are not true believers can show signs of Christianity which seem very much like the work of God's holy Spirit. The holy Spirit brings us to repentance, and many people can seem to be sorry for their sins. The holy Spirit teaches us the truth about Jesus, and such people do seem eager to learn about Christ. In the same way the holy Spirit leads us to do good deeds, and lots of people want to do good. The question, though, is how we view these signs of Christianity. What value do we place on doing good, or learning about Christ, or being sorry for sin? Do we think that these things can earn us God's forgiveness? People who are not real Christians think so. They think that their own sorrow for sins, or what they have learnt about Jesus, or their own good deeds — with, perhaps, some help from God — will earn them God's mercy. No *true* believer thinks like that. Every believer knows that only Jesus Christ can bring us to God.

There are three important and necessary things in Christianity. The first is, being emptied of all our own goodness, broken hearted, knowing we are sinners, lost and far from God (for Christ came to seek and save the lost). The second is being entirely satisfied with Jesus Christ as the only Saviour of lost sinners, and the third is turning whole-heartedly and completely to Jesus Christ, to do his will and to please him. Can you say, 'Yes: those three things are true of me'? These are the things which show that someone is a true Christian believer.

6.
Dealing with doubts about our faith

A true Christian believer values the Lord Jesus Christ above everything else. Christians know that they are sinners, lost and far away from God. Knowing that they have nothing good in themselves to bring to God, they turn wholeheartedly and entirely to Jesus Christ, to do his will and to please him. Do these things describe you?

Perhaps you're still not certain. At times you think you're a true Christian. Then at other times you seem so hopelessly sinful that you wonder if God's new life really is in you.

Sin in our lives can sometimes cause us to doubt whether we are Christians. Yet, in the Bible, we find believers trusting in God — even when sin seemed to be strong in their lives. Read Romans 7:24-25, where Paul thanks God through Jesus Christ, even though he is sad because sin still overcomes him. In Psalm 65:3 we read 'Sins overcame us; but as for our evil-doings, you, Lord, will clear them away'. Sin was there – but so was trust in God's power to make clean and to forgive. So sin in our lives does not have to make us doubt that we are Christians. Some sins begin with our human weaknesses, and come upon us unexpectedly, although we do not want to sin. At other times we intend to sin: and these sins contain all kinds of other evils mixed in with them. We must make a distinction here. Unexpected sins, sins that come from our natural human weakness, will always trouble the Christian. But sins which we want to do, and which bring other kinds of wrongdoing along with them, make it very hard to see whether a person is a true Christian. Nevertheless, when we turn away, even from serious, deliberate sins against God, we regain the sense of being true believers. After David had sinned against God by numbering the Israelites, he repented of this sin; David's conscience was troubled after he had counted the fighting men. And he said to the Lord, 'I have sinned greatly in what I have done. Now, O Lord, I beg you, take away the guilt of your servant' (2 Samuel 24:10). Notice that David calls himself God's servant here. Even though he has sinned deliberately, and been foolish, when he turns from that sin, he once again knows that he is a true believer.

But what about those unexpected sins, which come into our lives because we are naturally weak and sinful? Let's think again of what Paul says in Romans chapter 7. Certainly Paul knows that he is a sinner, yet he also thinks of himself as a believer. Paul knows that he fails to keep all God's law; yet he does not blame God's law — he blames himself as a sinner. Paul is also clear that he wants to do good, to keep all God's law, and to turn away from all evil. He says in Romans 7:19, 'I want to do good, but I do not do good. I want to keep from evil, but I do evil'. Thirdly, Paul feels sin as a burden — he does not like it in any way, and he wants to be free from it (Romans 7:24). Then Paul says that even while he is under the power of sin, there is still something in him which is fighting against it — and he's glad when that struggle ends in victory over sin (Romans 7:22-25).

So my question is, are you like Paul when you find sin unexpectedly getting the better of you? Do you blame yourself, not God's law, when you fail? Have you set yourself against sin and do you want to do good? Is there something in you which fights against sin, and which is glad when you do God's will? If so, sin may get the better of you when you least expect it, but you can still think of yourself as a believer. Yet, be warned: avoid sin and fight against it — for the more you do so, the more certain you will be of God's love for you. Paul said, 'The life which I live in this body, I live by faith in the Son of God who loved me and gave himself for me' (Galatians 2:20).

Some people doubt whether they are Christians for a different reason. They do not doubt because of sin; they doubt because they do not have the special sense of God's love or the special help of the holy Spirit, which some Christians seem to enjoy. Some people can tell of wonderful ways in which God has worked in their lives — God seems especially real to these people. But others seem not to have these blessings, and because they lack them, they begin to ask if they are Christians at all.

If you are like that, let me tell you that all Christians do, I believe, have many special blessings from the holy Spirit. Do you want to be holy? When you think about the holiness, goodness and purity of God, do you want something of that holiness to be in you, also? Well, if you do, that is a gift from the holy Spirit to you.

Do you feel that you have a special interest in God, and that God has a special interest in you? Is there a kind of sharing between yourself and God? And does the sense that you belong to God and that God is your God, become specially strong when you worship God? That, too, is a special gift from the holy Spirit.

Or again: do you know that you live in God's sight, and do you want to live and work knowing that God sees and knows you? Can you say, in the words of the Psalmist 'I have set the Lord always before me'? (Psalm 16:8). Do you sometimes feel something of God's presence with you? This too is a special gift from the Holy Spirit.

Certainly, some Christians have a very special sense, sometimes, of being with God, and of God's help. Enoch was like this. 'He walked with God' (Genesis 5:24). But every Christian has *some* sense of God's presence, and that is a gift from the holy Spirit.

Again — do you feel free to come to God? Do you feel as if there is nothing standing between yourself and God? Perhaps you do not always, or often, feel like this. But at the very least you know that Jesus Christ has cleared the way for you to come to God. You may not know the special experience of speaking freely to God in prayer, with great confidence. Some have this blessing, others do not. Yet all believers have something of God's gift of freedom — and we can do much ourselves to gain the enjoyment of speaking freely to God.

Do you know the holy Spirit's influence in your life? In an ordinary way, the holy Spirit must work like this in every believer, to keep each Christian alive to God. But there is a special working of the holy Spirit, when he stirs up our spiritual life and strengthens it. Not everyone knows this special working of the holy Spirit — but the same holy Spirit is at work in every believer.

Do you know that God hears your prayers? Occasionally believers know that God has heard them because he gives them a direct assurance that he has done so. This will probably not happen very often, yet every believer knows that God hears prayer. Moreover when we pray to God through Christ with faith, and without sinful motives, we can believe that God hears us. 1 John 5:14 tells us that if we ask anything that is in agreement with God's will, he hears us. If we know that God hears us in this way, then his holy Spirit has shown this to us.

Are you sure of God's favour towards you? This is something we can test without any special experiences. For example, 1 John 3:18-19 tells us that if we love other Christians in our actions and in truth, we may 'set our hearts at rest before God'. Love for other Christians is a sign of God's love in us, and we need no special experience to understand this. If we love other Christians, we can be sure of God's love for us. Sometimes, though, the holy Spirit shows believers in a special way that they have the signs of God's life in themselves. The holy Spirit makes them see clearly that something in their lives is God's work in them, and not their own work. Not all Christians have this special assurance of God's work in their lives. Nor do all Christians have another experience which is very hard to describe: the feeling of the presence of God in us, the sense of his love in our hearts, and the glory of God filling our whole beings. Such an experience is God's special gift to some believers for some special purpose. Do not doubt your faith because you lack this special gift.

Do you know peace with God? Every believer is in a state of peace, for 'being justified by faith we have peace with God,' (Romans 5:1). Believers are not always at peace in themselves, for they may be sometimes troubled in their consciences. Yet all Christians are in a state of peace with God, even if they do not sometimes feel it. 'Who will bring any charge against those whom God has chosen? It is God who justifies' (Romans 8:33). This, too, is a gift of the holy Spirit.

Do you ever have an experience of feeling a special sense of joy in God? 'You believe in him and are filled with an inexpressible and glorious joy' (1 Peter 1:8). The holy Spirit can sometimes cause the believer to feel a strong sense of delight at God's friendship. This, too, is the Spirit's way of giving believers confidence that their faith is genuine.

One further point, in conclusion. Because the special experiences of the Spirit I have described may come and go, we may be tempted to doubt if they are truly of God. We need to know that such experiences usually coincide with some particular circumstances in life when we may need special comfort. I refer to times of special sorrow over sin, or times of persecution, or when facing some heavy responsibility for God (1 Peter 4:14).

I hope you can see, then, that the holy Spirit is continually at work in all true Christian — not just in those who have special experiences of God's love. What really matters is what we think of Jesus Christ. Is he more precious to us than anything else? Do we trust in him as the Saviour and Lord of our lives? Do we want to be holy, as he is? Faith in Jesus Christ, and holiness — these are wonderful gifts of the holy Spirit. If you know something of them, be thankful you lack nothing essential to making you a child of God!

Part 2 —
How to become a Christian

7.
(Guthrie's chapter 1, and part of 2)
What it means to come to Christ

I've been trying to describe the signs of a true Christian. In part one of this book I have written about three special signs, amongst others, which show whether someone is a real believer in Jesus Christ. Firstly, believers are emptied of all their own goodness — they know that they are sinners, and that, without Jesus Christ, they are lost and far from God. Secondly, believers are entirely satisfied with Jesus Christ as the only saviour of lost sinners. Jesus is all they need, and he is precious to them. In third place, believers are people who have turned whole-heartedly and completely to Jesus Christ, to do his will and to please him. I've mentioned many other signs of true belief in Jesus Christ — but these three are among the most important.

Perhaps, as you've read these things, you've realised that you don't have these signs of true belief in your life. Maybe you wouldn't even dare to claim these signs for yourself. Well, in my next few chapters I want to say things that I hope will help you. I want to help you come to this true belief in the Lord Jesus Christ. If you know you are not a true believer, then it is your duty to come to the Lord Jesus Christ. For it is through Jesus Christ that God saves sinners, and only through him will you be sure of God's love and forgiveness.

Before I begin to say what it means to trust Jesus Christ, there are a few things which I should make clear first of all. For example, when Adam sinned and ate the fruit which God told him not to eat, he brought death upon us all. Romans 5:12 tells us that by one man sin entered into the world, and death because of sin, and so death spread to all people, because all have sinned. We are all sinners — our human nature is sinful — because we come from Adam, whose sin affected and ruined us all.

Nevertheless, God planned to rescue people from sin and save them through Jesus Christ. Even to Adam and Eve God promised that God's Son, Jesus Christ, would defeat Satan and evil, for God told them that the seed of the woman would bruise the serpent's head (Genesis 3:15).

In conclusion, God has promised to be at peace with all who seek salvation from sin through Jesus Christ. All such people belong to a new agreement made between God and themselves through Jesus Christ — an agreement that God will put away their sins, and that they will become his people.

Even so, there have always been people who pretended to be God's people but were not so in their hearts. Throughout history, and today, there are people who understand that Jesus Christ is the only way to God, yet who do not really love and obey him, whatever they say. They may enjoy many of the benefits of Christianity, but they are not really changed inside. As Psalm 78 verse 37 says, their hearts are not right with God. There are few people who truly and honestly come to Jesus Christ as their saviour and Lord, for the Bible tells us that the road which leads to life is narrow and there are few that find it (Matthew 7:14). The Bible tells us, too, that many are called, but few are chosen (Matthew 20:16). If we think about these statements, we should want to be sure whether we belong to God's people.

Lastly, although it is true that God draws sinners to himself, it is also true that sinners come to Jesus Christ. The Bible speaks of both. We cannot avoid our duty to come to Jesus by saying that only the people chosen by God will come to him. The Bible calls on us to believe in Jesus Christ and to receive him: 'As many as received him, to them he gave power to become the sons of God'. Yet Philippians chapter 1 verse 29 makes it plain that it is *given to us* to believe. The power to believe in Jesus Christ, to receive him, is given to us from God; yet we ourselves are commanded to believe in Jesus and to receive him. 'Come to me, all you who are weary and burdened, and I will give you rest', Jesus said (Matthew 11:28).

I hope you can understand those few points first of all. I hope you can see that we ought to come to Jesus Christ and receive him. Even so, what does it mean, to accept Jesus Christ and agree to God's plan of salvation through him? Firstly, it means leaving behind any thoughts of saving ourselves from sin. We must realise that we are unable to regain God's friendship by ourselves. We have lost it by our sin. We cannot rescue ourselves from the wrath of God which is due to us. We must forget all about trying to earn God's favour for ourselves.

Then, secondly, we must value Jesus Christ as the only one who can give us new life and true happiness. We must realise that God points us to Jesus Christ as the only one who can stand between sinners like ourselves, and a holy God, and bring sinful people back to God. We must trust ourselves to Jesus Christ just as we are, relying on his mercy alone to help us and save us. This is called faith, or believing; it is receiving Christ or believing on his name, as John chapter 1 verse 12 puts it. And this is the second part of agreeing with God's plan of salvation.

Accepting Jesus Christ means two things. It means giving up every effort to put ourselves right with God, knowing that we can never earn God's forgiveness. Then it means turning to Jesus Christ, knowing that he is the only one who can bring us forgiveness and peace with God. He is the one whom God sent into the world to do this: to seek and to save what was lost.

Let me remind you that it is your duty to accept Jesus Christ in the sense that I have just explained it. If you want to be sure of salvation from sin, and if you want to be sure of God's favour, then you *must* come to Jesus Christ, knowing that he alone can give you peace with God.

God commands you to come to Christ. As we have seen already, Jesus himself said, 'Come to me, all you who are tired and burdened, and I will give you rest' (Matthew 11:28). 1 John chapter 3 verse 23 tells us that 'this is his command: to believe on the name of his Son Jesus Christ'. Keeping to this duty gives us the right to be called children of God, for as John's gospel chapter 1 verse 12 says, 'to as many as received him he gave power to become the sons of God, even to them that believe on his name.'

This is the only way to come to God. We are accepted by God only through Jesus Christ, God's beloved Son. It is all 'to the praise of his (God's) glorious grace, in which he has made us accepted in his beloved one (Jesus Christ)' (Ephesians 1:6). Whatever else we may have, if we do not receive Jesus Christ and accept God's way of salvation through him, then there is no hope for us — we are not saved from sin, we are not accepted by God, and nothing we do can please God. 'Without faith it is impossible to please God' (Hebrew 11:6). 'He who does not believe is condemned already, and shall not see life, but the wrath of God remains on him' (John 3:18, 36). If we do not believe that the only way to God is Jesus Christ who died at Jerusalem, whom the prophets foretold, and who was shown to be God's Son by his many mighty works — if we do not believe this, we shall die in our sins. Jesus himself said, 'If you do not believe that I am he, you shall die in your sins' (John 8:24).

So I must tell you that it is absolutely necessary to accept Jesus Christ as the saviour of sinners. Remember that without Jesus Christ you are lost — and that God says, 'whoever wishes, let him take the free gift of the water of life' (Revelation 22:17). Remember that God will not turn away anyone who wants to be saved from sin; for, as Hebrews chapter 7 verse 25 tells us, he is 'able to save completely those who come to God through him' (i.e. through, relying on, Jesus Christ).

8.

(Continuing Guthrie's chapter 2)
The importance of coming to Christ sincerely

In my last chapter I was explaining that we cannot save ourselves from sin. We must value Jesus Christ as the only one who can save us from sin. We must turn to Jesus Christ, knowing that he is the only one who can forgive us our sin and bring us peace with God. This is what we ought to do. It is our duty. God commands us to believe in the Lord Jesus Christ. 'This is his commandment, that we should believe on the name of his Son Jesus Christ.'

Now I want you to understand that we must not come to Jesus Christ carelessly or thoughtlessly. Just saying that we believe in him is not enough: we must mean what we say.

We must realise that we were born sinners against God, and disobedient to Him. By many actual sins, throughout life, we have lost God's favour. We have all sinned in particular ways — and we should know what these particular sins are. If we come to Jesus Christ and mean it, we must know that we are sinners, and feel ourselves guilty of particular sins,

We must know, too, that God is angry with sinners. God is against sinners because of their sinful nature and because of their particular sins, too. God is opposed to all sin, and to all sinners because of their sin. In the Bible God names many sins — such as disrespect for, and carelessness about God, impurity in our lives, and very many others. We cannot read the Bible without understanding that God is against our sins — and that he is angry with us because of them.

We must know, too, that we cannot buy peace with God, for we have nothing of our own with which to buy it. All our goodness is like dirty rags, as Isaiah chapter 64 verse 6 says. Not even praying, or giving to the poor, or anything we try to do for God, will buy us peace with God — for, as long as we are unforgiven, we do not do these things out of love for God, or in obedience to God, or for the glory of God.

We must know that, as sinners, we have no love for God, no reverence for him, no sorrow for sin, and no faith in Jesus Christ. Until we know these things, we will never bring our burden of sin to the Lord Jesus Christ, but will try to leave it somewhere else.

Now we need to know all these things — and not just to know them, but to take them to heart seriously. We must feel the weight of them, we must treat them as real and solemn facts — we must treat these serious truths more earnestly than anything else. We shall never have to think of anything more important than these things.

And if we do take these facts seriously, then I believe that we shall seek salvation from sin with all our hearts. We shall 'seek first the kingdom of God' (Matthew 6:33). One thing will be on our minds: how to be at peace with God — how to be saved from sin. If this is not the most important matter for us, can we really say that we know anything about sin, or God, or God's everlasting wrath against sin?

If we take what God tells us seriously, we shall be broken-hearted because of our sin, and hate ourselves for it. If we know that we have destroyed ourselves by our sins, we shall certainly be ashamed of ourselves.

We shall seek relief from our sin, too, once we are truly convinced that we are sinners. We shall seek relief from sin urgently, realising that peace with God is more important than anything else. We must run for safety somewhere, and we dare not wait — we must get to safety now!

But where shall we run if we want to be saved from sin? We need the holy Spirit of God to show us that all the salvation and all the goodness we need is in Jesus Christ. We must see that Jesus Christ, the sinless one, has suffered God's punishment for their sin in place of sinners. So justice has been done. Jesus has borne the anger of God against sin instead of sinners. By this, Jesus Christ has obtained forgiveness and peace with God for all who will trust in him.

We must understand too, that God is willing to be at peace with sinners through Jesus Christ. In fact, as we have already seen, God commands us to believe in the Lord Jesus Christ. 'This is his command: to believe on the name of his Son, Jesus Christ' (1 John 3:23). We must not question God's willingness to receive all who truly come to Jesus Christ.

At the same time, we must understand that in coming to Jesus, we need to break away from all evil. If we know we are doing something wrong, we must stop it, straight away, before we can rightly and truly believe in the Lord Jesus.

This is what it means to believe in Jesus Christ truly and rightly. We must realise that we are sinners, we must be aware of our sins, we must know that God is angry with sinners because of their sins, we must know that we cannot do anything to buy peace with God, and we must seek Jesus Christ with all our hearts, as the only one who can give us this peace. I'm not saying that everybody will know all these facts clearly and distinctly — yet I am saying that such things are usually true of people who rightly believe in Jesus.

But coming to Jesus in the right way means more than knowing certain things and taking them seriously. You see — believing in Jesus is something personal. It is something we must do for ourselves. Habakkuk chapter 2 verse 4 says, 'The righteous person shall live by his faith' Notice that: not by someone else's faith. The person who is made right with God will live through his own faith. It is true that faith is God's gift

— but we must, each one, use that gift for ourselves. Being a member of a church, or having Christian parents, will not save us. Only personal faith in Jesus Christ will save us from sin.

And that faith must be sincere, from the heart, 'It is with the heart that a person believes and is put right with God' (Romans 10:10). There must be a strong seeking for Jesus Christ in our hearts, if we are to believe in him truly and deeply.

At the same time we must use our minds to understand what we are doing when we come to Jesus Christ. We must understand that only Jesus can save us; and we must come to him because we know we need his forgiveness — not just to get out of the discomfort of some passing difficulty, or to gain some temporary help.

So we must come to Christ determined to reach him and rest in him. We must not allow *anything* to put us off. Our great aim must be to come to Christ, in faith, for ourselves.

And when we do come to Christ like that, there will be some sure results. Firstly we shall know that we are at one with God. We shall know, when we trust in Christ, that we belong to him, and to God the Father. We shall know that God is at work for our good, that he cares for us, feels for us, and is concerned about us. And we, too, shall want to speak to God, to open our hearts to him, and daily to seek his forgiveness and peace through Jesus Christ. We shall entrust all our life to God, knowing that he cares for us; and we shall ask good things for ourselves and for others from God.

These are some of the blessings that come from peace with God, through faith in our Lord Jesus Christ. Have you come to Jesus Christ, truly, honestly, sincerely? To do so gives honour to God, for it is to do what he has intended to be done by all who seek salvation, and it is to bring untold blessing to ourselves. These are the reasons why Satan works so hard to prevent us believing. I want to answer some of Satan's arguments in the next chapter.

9.

(Guthrie's chapter 3)
Problems that prevent people coming to Christ

Some people, I know, feel they *cannot* come to Jesus Christ —
and in this chapter I want to think about this. People give all
kinds of reasons for not believing in Jesus Christ. Perhaps you
feel you cannot believe in him. I want to think about some
reasons why people do not trust in Jesus. I hope you will see
that there is no reason against believing in him for ourselves.

Some people say, 'I am so bad that I could never claim to
believe in Jesus — it would be presumption for someone as bad
as me'. Well, it's true that we are all sinners and far, far away
from God in our sin; for God is completely pure and holy. In
spite of all that, we must remember that God *chose* to save
sinners: the Son of God came into the world to seek and save
the lost. In Jesus Christ, God himself made a way of peace
between himself and the worst of the sinners. So when we
believe in Jesus, we trust in what God has done to save us. We
are not to think that we are too bad — or too good — to have
anything to do with Jesus. God has made this way to save
sinners; and he it is who commands us to turn to Christ: 'this
is his command — to believe in the name of his Son, Jesus
Christ' (1 John 3:23).

'But', say some people, 'my sins are far worse than the sins
of others. I can see that, in general, God has made the way to
save sinners: but my sins are too great even for that'. Yet the
Bible tells of God forgiving very great sinners: Peter denied
Christ; Paul persecuted Christians; Jonah was angry against

God; David committed adultery — yet all these people were forgiven. When it comes to God's mercy, all sins are equal: for all sins need the same remedy — God's forgiveness through Jesus Christ. As Hebrews chapter 7 verse 25 says, 'Jesus is able to save completely all who come to God through him'. The *worst* sin of all is not to believe in Jesus Christ, when we hear about forgiveness through faith in Him. 'He who does not believe stands condemned already' (John 3:18). The Apostle Paul said, 'Here is a trustworthy saying, which deserves full acceptance: Christ Jesus came into the world to save sinners, of whom I am the worst' (1 Timothy 1:15). If the worst of sinners could say that — how can your sins keep you from turning to Jesus Christ?

Even so, someone might say, 'my sins are made worse by other evils — worse than the sins you have mentioned'. I do not think they are. All the sins I spoke of just now were made worse than they need have been. You may think your sin worse, because you knew about God and his holy laws. So did Paul and Peter, Jonah and David. You may have planned to do evil. So did David. Something very small may have caused you to sin. It was so with Peter and Jonah. You may have sinned in the same way, over and over again. Peter did so, too. Our sins cannot be made so bad that we can never find forgiveness. God has promised that he will not in any way cast out those who come to him through Jesus. Read the words of Jesus in John 6:37; 'Whoever comes to me I will never drive away'.

Someone else might say at this point, 'you have not named my sins; you have mentioned many great sins that were forgiven — but if you only knew my sins you could never be so sure that God would forgive me'. In reply, I simply ask you to think about these words from the Bible, which tell us that God is willing to forgive all kinds of sins. Look at Exodus chapter 34:7; 'God forgives evil, disobedience and sin'. Doesn't that include sins of all kinds? Look at Ezekiel chapter 18:21-

22, which tells us that if anyone turns from all his sins, they will not be remembered against him. Doesn't that apply to anyone? Look at Matthew 12:31; 'All kinds of sin and speaking against God shall be forgiven'. Doesn't that refer to all sorts of sin? All kinds of sins shall be forgiven! 'The blood of Jesus... cleanses us from *every* sin' (1 John 1:7). There is really no reason at all for your refusing to come to Jesus Christ.

Some people, however, will still say that they have gone beyond God's forgiveness. There are people who think they are guilty of the sin against the holy Spirit. They think that these words, from Matthew 12:31-32, apply to them: 'Whoever says anything against the Son of Man shall be forgiven; but whoever speaks against the holy Spirit shall not be forgiven, either in this world or in the world to come'. These words of Jesus are very serious: and some people do believe that they have sinned against the Holy Spirit and can never be forgiven.

I want to try to explain about this 'sin against the holy Spirit'. What does it mean?

Perhaps I can say first of all what this sin against the holy Spirit does not mean. The sin against the holy Spirit does not mean speaking against God when we are being treated cruelly or hurt in order to make us say wrong things against God. Some of the Christians whom Paul had persecuted did this: they were treated cruelly, and made to speak against God: but they were still believers. They said wrong things against God — but they were made to do so against their will. The same is true if we speak evil of God when we are suffering in some way, when we are ill and unable for a while to control the way we speak. Despite this, we are still believers. The same is true also when evil thoughts of God, which we do not want to have in our minds, come into our minds all the same. None of these things is the sin against the holy Spirit — for all the while, in our hearts, we still love God.

The sin against the holy Spirit does not mean hating, or even persecuting, what is good, while we truly think that it is bad. Paul persecuted Christians before he was converted; but he was forgive for this, because he persecuted Christians while he was an unbeliever, and did not know what was good. So hating what is right, before we know that it is right, is not the sin against the holy Spirit.

The sin against the holy Spirit does not mean being jealous of others because God is blessing them, or complaining about the way God has dealt with us. These sins were found in Jonah: he was angry when the people of Nineveh repented and when God was merciful to them; and he complained about the way God had treated him — yet Jonah was still one of the Lord's people.

The sin against the holy Spirit does not mean going far away from God and falling into great sins: for many believers have sinned greatly in this way. Peter even denied the Lord Jesus Christ, but he was forgiven.

Resisting the holy Spirit, grieving him, or ignoring him: none of these is the sin against the holy Spirit, for the Bible calls us to repent of these sins; if they were unforgivable how could we repent of them?

Trying to kill yourself, or indeed succeeding in doing so, are not sins against the holy Spirit. The jailer at Philippi wanted to kill himself, yet obtained forgiveness, as Acts 16 verses 27 and 34 explain.

All these sins are dreadful and deserve God's wrath if we do not repent of them; yet none of these is the unforgivable sin against the holy Spirit.

So what is this 'sin against the holy Spirit'? It is not one simple act of sin. It is a rejecting and opposing of God's way of salvation through Jesus Christ, which the holy Spirit shows us in the gospel. The sin against the holy Spirit is a wrong done against Jesus Christ, against his blood given for sinners, and against the holy Spirit who brings the news of forgiveness through the blood of Jesus Christ. Hebrews 6:4 to 6 speak of this sin: 'It is impossible for those who have tasted the heavenly gift and who have shared in the holy Spirit... if they fall away, to be brought back to repentance'. And Hebrews 10:26 & 29 tell us that if we deliberately keep on sinning after we have received the knowledge of the truth, no sacrifice for sins is left, for we have trampled the Son of God underfoot, treated his blood as an unholy thing, and insulted the holy Spirit. This is something done against the holy Spirit by a person who understands that Jesus Christ is the saviour of sinners and is the way to God. It is a sin against the holy Spirit when a person who has been shown by the Spirit the truth and the goodness of salvation through Christ deliberately spurns that truth. That is a sin against the holy Spirit, because that person then turns against all that the holy Spirit has shown him, and wilfully sets himself against it. Indeed, as Hebrews chapter 6 verse 6 says, 'they put Christ to open shame'.

This sin against the holy Spirit, then, can be plainly seen: it is the absolute refusal to accept that Jesus is God's way of salvation, because of a malicious hatred against God. And anyone who is repentant cannot have sinned like this, for the sin against the holy Spirit leaves us unrepentant and opposed to God. If you feel your need for Jesus Christ, and for salvation through him, no sin of yours is too great to keep you from him. Come to him now, earnestly, and you will never fear that your sin is too great to be forgiven.

10.
(Continuing Guthrie's chapter 3 and including chapter 4)
More problems preventing some from coming to Christ — and the conclusion of the whole.

In this chapter I want to look at some more reasons why people do not trust in Christ to save them from sin.

'I do not have the power to believe', say some people. 'Faith is God's gift: we cannot produce it ourselves'.

Well now; it is true that faith is God's gift, but at the same time, as I've tried to show earlier, God commands us to believe in the Lord Jesus Christ. In commanding this, God wants us to *realise* that we have no power to believe, and so to ask him for that power instead. Never forget that God has promised to give us a new heart — a new desire to please and obey him. God tells us in Ezekiel chapter 36 verse 37 that he will let his people ask him to do things for them. If you truly want to be saved, God will not fail to give you the power and the faith.

'But', say others, 'so many people who have believed in Jesus are sorry that their lives are so poor and show so little goodness. I don't want to be like them — fruitless and disappointing — so I don't feel I can come to Jesus Christ'.

Remember, though, that God still commands you to believe in Jesus Christ. It may be that some Christians have not made progress because of their small faith — but that is no reason for you not to trust in Jesus Christ. Even those who have made the smallest progress will surely agree that Christ is the source of every good thing, and that he has welcomed them with rich blessings, as Psalm 21 verse 3 puts it.

Some people, though, say they are confused about trusting in Jesus Christ. They say that sometimes in the Bible, God seems to offer to be their God without any mention of Jesus Christ. yet at other times we are called to come to Christ himself. How are we to come to God?

It is true that, when God first created man, Adam was perfect and could come straight to God. But when Adam sinned, he went far away from God and was unable to get back to God. So God made a new way for sinners to come back to him — the way of faith in Jesus Christ, the saviour of sinners. We read about Jesus, 'he is able to save completely those who come to God through him' (Hebrew 7:25). So when God calls us back to himself, he means us to come by the only way we can — by trusting in Jesus Christ. 'This is my Son, whom I love; with him I am well pleased. Listen to him!' (Matthew 17:5).

I hope you can see that there is nothing to stop any sinner from turning to Christ to be saved from sin. In fact there is every reason to turn to Jesus Christ now. God commands it; he will condemn all who do not turn to Jesus Christ; and our only hope of peace with God, forgiveness of sin and everything good and holy, is in Jesus Christ.

I hope that you are a true believer in the Lord Jesus Christ. I hope that you have seen how God saves sinners through Jesus Christ, that you want Jesus Christ more than anything else, that you value him as the only saviour of sinners, and that you are enjoying peace with God through him.

I realise, though, that many true Christians sometimes wonder, later on, if they really have trusted in Jesus Christ for themselves. It is very easy to begin doubting whether we have truly believed.

So as I finish this chapter may I suggest something which

I hope will help you, if you are a true believer in the Lord Jesus Christ. Quite definitely, clearly, speaking it out aloud, tell God that you agree to God's way of salvation through the Lord Jesus, and so make your acceptance of his salvation plain. Of course, nobody has to do this in order to be saved: the important thing is to believe in the Lord Jesus Christ in our hearts, sincerely. Even so, I think that stating that you believe like this will help and strengthen you as a Christian. It will make clear to you that there is a definite agreement between yourself and God, and so will help to strengthen your faith and settle you in a godly way of life.

Before I go any further let me show you that there are good reasons from the Bible, for saying deliberately, out loud, that you agree to God's way of salvation through Jesus Christ. Many bible passages talk of God's people stating that they belong to him. Think of Isaiah chapter 44 verse 5: 'One shall say, 'I am the Lord's'; or of Zechariah chapter 13:9, 'They shall say, 'The Lord is our God.' When Jesus, after he had risen from the dead, showed himself to Thomas who had doubted, Thomas said to him, 'My Lord and my God.' (John 20:28). We make sure we put things clearly when we do business, or make some agreement with another person. When a man and a woman marry, their agreement is spoken openly and deliberately. Silent consent of the heart does not make a legal union. In addition the relationship between a believer and Christ is, in the Bible, sometimes compared to a marriage. The most important thing we can ever do is to believe on the Lord Jesus Christ. Should we not express our personal belief in him most clearly and plainly? After all, God speaks plainly to us. Everything God has done to save sinners has been made perfectly exact, clear and plain.

So how should we put our faith in Jesus Christ into words? First, we should do so confidently. No doubt our words will be imperfect: they cannot express all we want to say. Yet

2 Corinthians chapter 8 verse 12 reminds us that, when we have a willing mind, God accepts whatever we can do, even though it does not seem enough to us.

Secondly, we should express our faith in a holy way. We should not say we believe in the Lord Jesus without taking great care: we speak to the Lord God who is holy. So we need to make time first to confess our sins and to fill our minds with thoughts of God's greatness and power. Remember how David spoke to God; 'You are great, O Lord God, for there is none like you nor is there any God besides you,' (2 Samuel 7:22). In this state of mind we should tell God that we accept for ourselves his way of saving sinners through Jesus Christ, and that we trust in Jesus Christ alone for salvation.

We need to be careful once we have put our personal faith into words like this. If we go away from God, having said that we trust in Jesus Christ, our consciences will be troubled. So we need to keep to all that we have said and hold firmly to all we believe, against every enemy. For it is a shame for anyone who has submitted to God's way of salvation, and who has said so, to say or do anything against God.

I hope you can see that there is great value in saying out aloud before God that we trust in Jesus Christ. It is right that we should clearly and definitely say that left to ourselves we are lost, far from God, and guilty before him; that Jesus Christ is the only one who can save us and bring us back to God, and that we accept this way of salvation, are thankful for it, satisfied with it, and trust ourselves entirely to God, to be saved in his way. It will mean very much to us if we are sure that God knows of a day and time when we accepted peace with God through Jesus Christ, and came to God to be his people, living in obedience to him. You may not always feel as much love for God as you would like; remember that in those to whom God gives a new spiritual life, there still also remains something of the sinful nature.

Yet if you know you need the Lord Jesus — speak to God like this. You may fear that you will go away from God; even so, what else can you do but come to his way of salvation, since there is no other! If you are sure that Jesus Christ alone can save, speak to God like this. You may feel that there are few signs of God's life within you, yet remember that this is because of your own unbelief and carelessness, not because God is unwilling to receive you. God is ready to receive all who come to him; he commands us to go to Jesus Christ and accept his salvation.

Oh! how I long to persuade people to believe that all these things are true, so they hurry to Christ, who himself is coming to judge the world concerning their attitude to these very truths!